SCHOLASTIC

Reading Passages
That Build Comprehension

INFERENCE

BY LINDA WARD BEECH

NEW YORK • TORONTO • LONDON • AUCKLAND • SYDNEY
MEXICO CITY • NEW DELHI • HONG KONG • BUENOS AIRES

Teaching *Resources*

Contents

Cover design by Maria Lilja
Interior design by Holly Grundon
Interior art by Mike Gordon

ISBN 0-439-55424-1
Copyright © 2005 by Linda Ward Beech.
All rights reserved.
Printed in the U.S.A.

7 8 9 10   40   14 13 12 11 10 09

Introduction

Reading comprehension involves numerous thinking skills. Making inferences is one of them. A reader who is adept at making inferences makes better sense of a text and increases his or her understanding of what is being communicated. Most primary school students don't know what an inference is. However, many of them are probably already making inferences—both in their reading and in their daily lives—without being aware of it. This book will help you help students learn to make inferences and to use them in their reading. Use the pages that follow to teach this skill to students and to give them practice in employing it.

Using This Book

Pages 5-7

After introducing inferences to students (see page 4), duplicate and pass out pages 5–7. Use page 5 to help students review and practice what they have just learned about making inferences. By explaining their thinking, students are using metacognition to analyze how they made their inferences. Pages 6–7 give students a model of the practice pages to come. They also provide a model of the thinking students might use in choosing the best sentence for making an inference from the paragraph.

Page 8

Use this page as a pre-assessment to find out how students think when they make an inference. Although answers are given on page 48, you'll want to acknowledge any responses that make sense. For example, in the first item, most students will say that Sami didn't want to be alone because he had watched a scary movie; however, some students might say that Sami watched a sad movie. When going over these pages with students, discuss why some inferences are better than others and why some are incorrect or do not make sense.

Pages 9-43

These pages offer practice in making inferences. The first paragraph on each page is a nonfiction passage similar to one students might encounter in a social studies or science text. The second paragraph is a fictionalized passage similar to one they might find in a reading book. After reading each paragraph, students should fill in the bubble in front of the correct answer for each question.

Pages 44-46

After they have completed the practice pages, use these pages to assess the way students think when they make inferences. Explain that students should use the illustration as well as the text and their own knowledge to answer the questions.

Page 47

You may wish to keep a record of students' progress as they complete the practice pages. Sample comments that will help you guide students toward improving their skills might include:
- reads carelessly
- misunderstands text
- doesn't apply own knowledge
- lacks background to make correct inference

Teacher Tip

For students who need extra help, you might suggest that they keep pages 5–7 with them to use as examples when they complete the practice pages.

Mini-Lesson: Teaching Inference Skills

1. Introduce the concept: Write these words on the chalkboard:

Miranda is sick today.

Ask students which of the following sentences best goes with the statement.

○ A. Miranda will stay home from school today.

○ B. Miranda's uncle is a dentist.

2. Model thinking: After students have correctly identified **A** as the sentence that best goes with the statement, explore why they chose this answer by modeling how they might think aloud.

Very often when someone is sick, that person stays home from school or work. I know this because I have stayed home when I was ill.

If you are sick, you would most likely go to a doctor, not a dentist. So the fact that Miranda's uncle is a dentist is probably not related to her illness.

3. Define the skill: Explain to students that a text doesn't always include every fact or detail about something. Often the reader has to add more information. When a reader adds information that he or she already knows to what is stated, the reader is making an inference.

Information in the Text	What the Reader Knows
Miranda is sick.	People stay home when they are sick.

4. Practice the skill: Use Practice Pages 9–43 to give students practice in making inferences.

Name_____ Date_____

What Is an Inference?

You read a story. You get some information. But often a story does not tell every detail about a subject. What does a reader do then? A good reader thinks about the information. A reader might think:

What else do I know about this subject?

How does what I know fit with what I have read?

By filling in missing information, a reader makes an **inference**.
An inference is a kind of guess.

Read the paragraph below, and then answer the questions.

Time for Breakfast

Dad called Connie. There was no answer. Then Mom went to the door of Connie's room. She called too. "Breakfast is ready," said Mom. There was still no answer.

What facts are given in this story?

1. Dad called Connie but

   there was no answer.

2. Breakfast was ready but

   _____

   _____ .

Make an inference.

3. What time of day is it?

   _____

4. How do you know?

   _____

5. What is Connie probably doing?

   _____

6. Why do you think so?

   _____

When you make an inference, use the facts that are given. Use what you know. Put the information together. Ask yourself whether your inference makes sense.

Name _____ Date _____

Making Inferences

Study these two pages. They show how a student made inferences.

Read the paragraph. Then fill in the
bubble that best answers the question.

Cave Explorers

Do you know what a potholer is? A potholer is someone who explores caves. To be safe from falling rocks, a potholer wears a hard hat. Down into the cave he or she goes. Sometimes a potholer has to crawl. Sometimes he or she must climb. It is often wet in a cave.

Which sentence is most likely true?

○ A. A potholer never
walks in a cave.

It doesn't say that a potholer never walks. I think that people sometimes walk in caves.

○ C. A potholer's work is
very safe.

It says there are falling rocks. That's not so safe. I don't think it is safe if you have to crawl and climb either.

● B. A potholer gets
dirty on the job.

You **could** get dirty crawling and climbing. I usually do. Also, it says the cave is wet.

I am going to fill in **B**. This sentence makes the most sense. I think you can guess that being a potholer could be a dirty job.

Making Inferences

Read the paragraph. Then fill in the
bubble that best answers the question.

Sally's Snack

Sally dashed from the elevator. She gave her grandmother a quick hug at the door. She dropped her book bag on the table. Then Sally headed for the kitchen. Out came the bread. Out came the jam. In no time Sally made a snack.

Which sentence is most likely true?

○ A. Sally does not have any homework.

◉ C. Sally is hungry after school.

It doesn't say anything about homework. But kids usually have some in their book bags. Also I think Sally just came home from school.

Sally rushed in the door with a book bag. She most likely came from school. She only gave her grandmother a quick hug. Then she went to the kitchen and got a snack. Most kids do the same thing.

○ B. Sally likes peanut butter on bread.

It doesn't mention peanut butter although that often goes with jam.

I am going to fill in **C.** This sentence makes the best sense. Sally is in a hurry to eat something. The book bag makes me think she has come from school.

Name_____ Date_____

Thinking About Information

Read each set of sentences. Then answer the questions.

1. Sami watched a movie. He did not want to be alone after it was over.

   Why does Sami feel this way?

   _____

   _____

   Why do you think so?

   _____

   _____

2. Max read the newspaper. He cheered when he found last night's score.

   What part of the paper is Max reading?

   _____

   _____

   Why do you think so?

   _____

   _____

3. The men slid down a pole. In no time they drove away in their truck.

   Who are the men?

   _____

   _____

   Why do you think so?

   _____

   _____

4. Betty wore a cast on one leg. She used crutches when she walked.

   What happened to Betty?

   _____

   _____

   Why do you think so?

   _____

   _____

Practice Page 1

Name_____   Date_____

Read each paragraph. Then fill in the bubble
that best answers each question.

The Factory

The factory was humming. On one floor a metal press stamped a large square of blue nylon. Fifty white stars appeared on the cloth. A worker stitched the stars more firmly in place. Then the blue square was attached to 13 stripes of red and white nylon. Finally, the worker folded the whole thing into a box.

1. **Which sentence is most likely true?**

   ○ A. The workers in this factory make nylon.

   ○ B. This paragraph is about making music.

   ○ C. This paragraph is about a flag factory.

Max Makes a Call

Max picked up the telephone and began to dial. Frowning, he put down the receiver. He opened a drawer in the desk and pulled out a large book. Max turned the pages. Soon he found what he was looking for. Then Max picked up the phone and dialed once more.

2. **Which sentence is most likely true?**

   ○ A. Max was making a long distance call.

   ○ B. Max forgot the number he was calling.

   ○ C. Max forgot what he wanted to say.

Practice Page 2

Name_____ Date_____

Read each paragraph. Then fill in the bubble
that best answers each question.

Meet Stegosaurus

Stegosaurus was an interesting-looking dinosaur. It had large plates shaped like triangles along its back. However, Stegosaurus had a very small head. Stegosaurus also had weak jaws. It had no teeth in the front of its jaws. It could not tear through tough skin. Stegosaurus ate things it found on the ground.

1. **Which sentence is most likely true?**
   ○ A. Stegosaurus was a plant-eating dinosaur.
   ○ B. Stegosaurus had teeth shaped like triangles.
   ○ C. Stegosaurus used its mouth for protection.

What the Wens Did

On Saturday, the Wens parked in the huge lot. They walked to the big building. Inside, they passed many stores. They stopped to buy shoes for Carl. They looked in the windows of a watch shop. Mrs. Wen bought some perfume in another store. Mr. Wen tried on a belt. By lunchtime, everyone was ready to wait in line at the snack shop.

2. **Which sentence is most likely true?**
   ○ A. The Wens are doing Saturday chores.
   ○ B. The Wens are shopping at a mall.
   ○ C. The Wens can't afford costly things.

Scholastic Teaching Resources   *Reading Passages That Build Comprehension: Inference*

Practice Page 3

Name_____ Date_____

Read each paragraph. Then fill in the bubble
that best answers each question.

Owl Features

Did you know that owls have ears? In fact, owls have large ears that are good for listening to night sounds. Owls also have big eyes that see well in the dark. Owls have big wings too. These large wings don't make loud flapping noises when an owl flies after its dinner.

Shhhh!

1. **Which sentence is most likely true?**

   ○ A. Owls can quietly hunt for food at night.

   ○ B. Owls are thoughtful about other animals.

   ○ C. Owls are careless about making noise.

Making a Decision

Mrs. Elliot looked at a lot of samples. She brought many of them home. She held them up in different parts of the living room. She asked all the members of the family to name their favorite. She called her friends and asked their opinions as well. Finally, she made a decision. Mrs. Elliot called the painter the next day.

2. **Which sentence is most likely true?**

   ○ A. Mrs. Elliot has a large group of friends.

   ○ B. The Elliot family has a big living room.

   ○ C. Mrs. Elliot is having her living room painted.

Practice Page 4

Name_____ Date_____

Read each paragraph. Then fill in the bubble
that best answers each question.

Elvis

Elvis works in a hospital in San Francisco. Elvis's job is to carry medicine from place to place. But Elvis is no ordinary worker. For one thing, Elvis weighs 600 pounds. Elvis also has wheels instead of feet. When told where to go, Elvis chugs down hallways, gets on elevators, and never bumps into anything.

1. Which sentence is most likely true?

- ○ A. Elvis needs to lose weight.
- ○ B. Elvis is a hospital robot.
- ○ C. Elvis is a friendly worker.

What a Mess

The jar fell off the shelf and crashed to the floor. Red sauce sprayed everywhere. Pieces of glass flew around too. Christine looked at the mess with wide eyes. Would she have to pay for the broken jar? She paused and wondered what to do. Then Christine left her cart and went looking for the manager.

2. Which sentence is most likely true?

- ○ A. Christine was injured by the broken jar.
- ○ B. Christine broke the jar by accident.
- ○ C. Someone threw a jar at Christine.

Scholastic Teaching Resources   *Reading Passages That Build Comprehension: Inference*

Practice Page 5

Name_____ Date_____

Read each paragraph. Then fill in the bubble
that best answers each question.

All About Camels

Do you know what a ship of the desert is?
It is a camel. These animals are good for
carrying people and supplies across hot, dry
deserts. Camels can go many days without
getting thirsty. Camels can also go for a long
time without food. They
live off the fat in their
humps when there is
no food.

1. Which sentence is most likely true?

  ○ A. Camels eat sand most of the time.

  ○ B. Camels don't like to eat or drink.

  ○ C. The desert has little food or water.

Kim at Work

The sun was warm on her back, so
Kim took off her sweatshirt. She
picked up the shovel and turned over
the soil. She spread some fertilizer in
the freshly dug earth. Then Kim made
narrow rows and sprinkled in seeds.
How long would it take for these
flowers to grow, she wondered.

**2. Which sentence is most
likely true?**

  ○ A. Kim is admiring her
garden.

  ○ B. It is a day in spring.

  ○ C. It is the end of summer.

Practice Page 6

Name_____ Date_____

Read each paragraph. Then fill in the bubble
that best answers each question.

Meet Eric Carle

Perhaps you have read *The Very Hungry Caterpillar*. This book is by Eric Carle. He is also the author of *The Very Quiet Cricket*. Another book that Carle wrote is *A House for Hermit Crab*. Before he writes a book, Carle learns a lot about his subject. What do you think he learned about when he wrote *The Tiny Seed*?

1. **Which sentence is most likely true?**
   - ○ A. Eric Carle writes books about nature.
   - ○ B. Eric Carle has some unusual pets.
   - ○ C. Eric Carle only writes about animals.

Neil and His Book

Neil rubbed his eyes and yawned. He was thinking about the television program he'd seen last night. As his eyes closed, Neil's head drooped to his chest. Then a noise made him jump. Startled, Neil tried to read the page in his book again. If only he could take a nap.

2. **Which sentence is most likely true?**
   - ○ A. Neil is reading an exciting book.
   - ○ B. Neil stayed up too late last night.
   - ○ C. Neil watched a noisy TV program.

Practice Page 7

Name_____ Date_____

Read each paragraph. Then fill in the bubble
that best answers each question.

Trouble in the Pacific

A loud roar came from an island in the Pacific Ocean. Fiery rock and smoke shot into the sky. People 3,000 miles away heard the noise. Dust hung in the air. Great waves rolled through the sea. They slammed into villages along the coasts of other islands. The damage was huge.

1. Which sentence is most likely true?

○ A. A dragon on the island was angry.

○ B. There was a blizzard on the island.

○ C. A volcano erupted on the island.

In the Display Case

The little boy stood on tiptoe to see inside the display case. He pointed to one of the containers. As the clerk opened the case, the little boy shook his head. He looked some more. He pointed to another container. But, no, that wasn't the one either. Finally, the little boy nodded and pointed to still another container. The smiling clerk began scooping.

2. Which sentence is most likely true?

○ A. The boy is trying to make the clerk angry.

○ B. The boy is choosing an ice cream flavor.

○ C. The store does not have many choices.

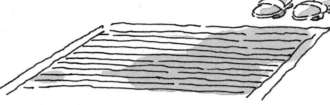

Practice Page 8

Name_____ Date_____

Read each paragraph. Then fill in the bubble
that best answers each question.

Be Careful About Customs

You have to be careful about customs. Not everyone follows the same ones. For example, in Japan people remove their shoes before entering a temple. They don't let their socks touch the floor. Instead, they step directly onto a mat called a *tatami*. Many visitors don't know this custom. So sometimes they seem rude.

1. Which sentence is most likely true?

○ A. People in Japan go barefoot most of the time.

○ B. Foreigners might not remove shoes at a temple.

○ C. People in Japan think shoes and socks are silly.

Leaving Home

Mr. Patel was ready to leave for the day. He kissed his wife and children goodbye. He gave the dog a pat on the head. Then he picked up his briefcase and opened the door. Stepping outside, Mr. Patel looked up. He held out his hand. Quickly, he turned around and went back into the house.

2. Which sentence is most likely true?

○ A. Mr. Patel wants to say goodbye again.

○ B. Mr. Patel forgot to pat the cat.

○ C. Mr. Patel went back to get an umbrella.

Practice Page **9**

Name_____ Date_____

Read each paragraph. Then fill in the bubble
that best answers each question.

On the River

All year long, powerful tugboats push barges up and down the Hudson River. The barges are loaded with oil, gas, and supplies for factories. In the winter of 2003, the tugboats and barges often got stuck. They had to be rescued by icebreakers. First a breaker would free the frozen boats. Then it would cut a path through the frozen water. Then the river traffic could move again.

1. **Which sentence is most likely true?**

   ○ A. The winter of 2003 had low temperatures.

   ○ B. Tugboats and barges got stuck in the mud.

   ○ C. Not much happens on the river in winter.

Busy Nan

Nan opened the drawer and took out five forks. She counted out knives and spoons too. Then she got water glasses and plates down from the cabinet. She folded some napkins and found her little brother's bib. Nan even remembered to get out the salt and pepper.

2. **Which sentence is most likely true?**

   ○ A. Nan is going to have a tea party.

   ○ B. Nan works in a large restaurant.

   ○ C. Nan is setting the table for supper.

Practice Page 10

Name_____ Date_____

Read each paragraph. Then fill in the bubble
that best answers each question.

The Arrival

A cargo plane lands at the airport
in the middle of the night. By
5:30 A.M. the valuable cargo is on a
truck. An hour after that, a painting is
carefully unpacked in a
large building. Specially
trained experts check to be
sure that the artwork is in
good condition. Later that
day the painting will be one
of many hanging in a gallery.

1. Which sentence is most likely true?

○ A. The painting is to be in an airport exhibit.

○ B. The painting was sent for an art show.

○ C. The painting was not packed very well.

Karl Gets Up

K arl sat and gazed at the view. He
could see some of his friends in the
distance. Lazily, he moved his feet back
and forth in the sand. It felt fine and
warm. Karl was so comfortable, it was
almost too much trouble to get up. But that
was why he was here. Suddenly, he stood
and yelled "Here I come!" Then he ran
toward the water.

2. Which sentence is most likely true?

○ A. Karl is at the beach.

○ B. It is a windy day.

○ C. Karl is in the desert.

Scholastic Teaching Resources   *Reading Passages That Build Comprehension: Inference*

Practice Page 11 Name_____ Date_____

Read each paragraph. Then fill in the bubble
that best answers each question.

Numbers

The earliest people didn't have numbers. They probably knew that there were more of some things than others. But people wanted to keep track of what they had. How many sheep did they have? How many spears? At first people made marks on a stick or wall to count things. Later they invented symbols for different amounts. We call these numbers.

1. **Which sentence is most likely true?**
   ○ A. People invented numbers to keep records.
   ○ B. People had too many things to count.
   ○ C. People had no reason to count things.

Dale's Day

Dale sat at his desk and sharpened a pencil. He stared at the blank pad. No ideas. Sighing, Dale played with his eraser. He looked out the window. He gazed around his room. Maybe a snack would help. Dale ran down to the kitchen for some cookies. Then he called his friend Jack to talk about the assignment. By six o'clock, Dale was getting worried.

2. **Which sentence is most likely true?**
   ○ A. Jack will do the assignment for Dale.
   ○ B. Dale can't get started writing.
   ○ C. Dale finds it easy to write papers.

Practice Page 12

Name_____ Date_____

Read each paragraph. Then fill in the bubble
that best answers each question.

Damage in Pierce City

As the reporters pulled into Pierce City, they couldn't believe all the damage they saw. It seemed to follow a path right through the town. Trees along the road were uprooted. A roof was missing from one house. Two cars were upside down in someone's yard. And in a trailer park, several homes had been blown over.

1. **Which sentence is most likely true?**
   - ○ A. The town was struck by lightning.
   - ○ B. The town was really a movie set.
   - ○ C. The town was hit by a bad tornado.

Mr. Bruno's Ride

Mr. Bruno slowed down as he came to the toll. Traffic was heavy, and there were lines of cars in front of him. Slowly, he inched forward. At last he was through the entrance. He drove carefully, staying in his lane and away from the walls. After a mile and a half, he was out in the open again. He was glad to see the sky overhead.

2. **Which sentence is most likely true?**
   - ○ A. Mr. Bruno is driving over a bridge.
   - ○ B. Mr. Bruno is going through a tunnel.
   - ○ C. Mr. Bruno is at an amusement park.

Name_____ Date_____

Read each paragraph. Then fill in the bubble
that best answers each question.

Animal Colors

Animals have different forms of protection.
Often they look like their surroundings.
This is called camouflage. Polar bears live in
cold regions. Their white fur blends in with the
snow. Lions are a tan color
much like the grasslands
where they live. Some
caterpillars are green during
the summer months. In the
fall they turn brown like the
branches they live on.

1. Which sentence is most likely true?

○ A. All animals are difficult to see.

○ B. All animals change colors.

○ C. Color is a form of camouflage.

What Jake Did

Jake held his breath. His head
moved back and forth as he
followed the acrobat. His neck hurt from
looking up into the top of the tent. For a
long moment, his hand paused over the
bag of popcorn he held. Finally, the
acrobat landed safely. Jake cheered in
relief and began eating again.

2. Which sentence is most likely true?

○ A. Jack is not having a good time.

○ B. Jake is at a circus show.

○ C. The popcorn isn't very tasty.

Name_____   Date_____

Read each paragraph. Then fill in the bubble
that best answers each question.

Road Signs

Drivers see many of the same
signs each time they are on the
road. One of the most common traffic
signs is "Stop." Another one is "Slow."
These two signs alone
prevent lots of accidents.
Some other helpful signs are
"Enter" and "Exit." The
road signs "Yield" and
"Caution" also provide
good advice.

1. **Which sentence is most likely true?**
   ○ A. Drivers do not obey traffic signs.
   ○ B. Road signs are hard to read.
   ○ C. Many road signs are for safety.

Words on a Wall

The students in Mr. Habib's class
were making a word wall. Alex
pinned up the word *rocket*. Erin got
out a dictionary to check on *shuttle*. Ed
and Macy wrote a sentence using *orbit*.
Nelson wanted to add *probe* to the wall,
and June planned to use *gravity*.

2. **Which sentence is most
likely true?**
   ○ A. Mr. Habib's class is
      making wallpaper.
   ○ B. The students are not
      very good spellers.
   ○ C. Mr. Habib's students are
      studying space.

Practice Page 15   Name_____   Date_____

Read each paragraph. Then fill in the bubble
that best answers each question.

Weaving

In many parts of the world,
women make rugs and blankets
on hand looms. They use
yarn spun from cotton or
wool. The yarn is dyed with
natural plant colors. The
designs that the women
weave are age-old. Often
the designs and colors have
special meaning to a region
or group of people.

1. **Which sentence is most likely true?**

   ○ A. All rugs and blankets are woven
   by women.

   ○ B. Weaving is a traditional art in
   many places.

   ○ C. The weaving industry never uses
   new designs.

Calling Dana

Dana and her parents sat in the first
row. Dana was a little nervous, but
her parents had big smiles on their faces.
Dana clapped politely as the principal
called out names. She watched different
students go to the stage. Then her name was
called! Excitedly, Dana went up on the
stage. She could hear her father cheering as
the principal held out his hand.

2. **Which sentence is
   most likely true?**

   ○ A. Dana is going to
   become an actress.

   ○ B. Dana has won an
   award at school.

   ○ C. Dana is in trouble
   with the principal.

Practice Page **16**

Name_____ Date_____

Read each paragraph. Then fill in the bubble
that best answers each question.

Paper Money

Have you ever looked closely at a five
dollar bill? Tiny red and blue fibers are
all over the paper. If you hold the bill up to the
light, you will see a picture.
It is called a watermark.
Each bill also has a number
that sparkles and changes
color. Another number is so
small, you need a magnifying
glass to read it. All these
things make U.S. paper
money hard to copy.

1. Which sentence is most likely true?

◯ A. No one ever tries to copy United
States paper money.

◯ B. The U.S. does not want anyone to
copy its money.

◯ C. You need a magnifying glass to use
U.S. money.

On the Steps

Jim was sitting on the steps to his house.
He was reading a book. He was also
waiting for his friends to come over. Suddenly,
something tickled Jim's arm. He scratched his
arm. A few minutes later it happened again.
This time Jim saw that an ant was crawling up
his arm. There were ants on the steps, too.

**2. Which sentence is
most likely true?**

◯ A. Jim is sitting
near an anthill.

◯ B. Jim's friends
brought ants.

◯ C. Jim was reading
about ants.

Practice Page 17

Name_____ Date_____

Read each paragraph. Then fill in the bubble
that best answers each question.

A Greek Word

In the Greek language *rhinos* means "nose." Can you see this Greek word in the English word *rhinoceros*? This animal certainly has a big nose! Other English words have *rhinos* in them, too. A rhinovirus might affect your nose. This virus is what people get when they have a cold.

-sniff-

1. **Which sentence is most likely true?**
   ○ A. A nose doctor is called a rhinologist.
   ○ B. A rhinoceros gets a lot of colds.
   ○ C. The Greek language is full of viruses.

Roger

Roger heard a noise. It was a car coming down the street. Even though he was taking a nap, Roger just had to see who it was. He padded over to the fence. It wasn't a car. It was a truck! Maybe it was the workman he had met yesterday. In a flash, Roger scampered out of his yard.

2. **Which sentence is most likely true?**
   ○ A. Roger is a neighborhood dog.
   ○ B. Roger is a friendly boy.
   ○ C. Roger is bored with workmen.

Practice Page **18**

Name_____ Date_____

Read each paragraph. Then fill in the bubble that best answers each question.

In Coober Pedy

Coober Pedy is a small mining town. It is in the southern part of Australia. The temperature there is usually 100 degrees in the summer. Some people in Coober Pedy have made their homes in old mines. They escape the heat by living in underground tunnels.

1. Which sentence is most likely true?

○ A. Coober Pedy has no regular houses.

○ B. It is cooler to live underground.

○ C. Miners prefer to live underground.

Getting Ready

Brian smeared white cream all over his face. He put on a round fake nose. He used red cream to make big spots on his cheeks. He painted on a big red smile, too. He used black to make up his eyes. Finally Brian put on a funny orange wig.

2. Which sentence is most likely true?

○ A. Brian is going to be a cat for Halloween.

○ B. Brian is protecting himself from the sun.

○ C. Brian will perform as a circus clown.

Practice Page 19

Name_____ Date_____

Read each paragraph. Then fill in the bubble that best answers each question.

In the Night

Most people do their sleeping during the day. But many wild creatures do not. Mice do much of their roaming at night. It's harder for foxes to hunt them in the dark. When otters live near people, they are more active at night. A dragonfly sheds its skin at night. It takes a few hours for the new adult's wings to grow strong. By morning the dragonfly is ready to fly away.

1. **Which sentence is most likely true?**

   ○ A. Otters like to live near people.

   ○ B. It is safer for some animals at night.

   ○ C. Wild animals have more fun at night.

What Happened?

One night something furry slipped from the hollow tree. A masked animal crept across the sidewalk. It stopped by a container. With little trouble, the animal got the lid off. Crash! The lid clattered to the ground. Mr. Tucker woke up and looked out the window. There was trash on the sidewalk. He could see a striped tail disappear around the corner.

2. **Which sentence is most likely true?**

   ○ A. A raccoon got into the garbage.

   ○ B. Mr. Tucker had a bad dream.

   ○ C. An animal robbed Mr. Tucker.

Practice Page **20**

Name_____ Date_____

Read each paragraph. Then fill in the bubble
that best answers each question.

Weather Vanes

Old weather vanes sit on the rooftops of some buildings. The vanes show the direction of the wind. The first vanes were also signs. Their designs told what people did. Farmers had vanes shaped like roosters or horses. A ship captain often had a whale design. George Washington had a special weather vane. It was a dove with an olive branch—two symbols of peace.

1. Which sentence is most likely true?

○ A. George Washington made the first weather vane.

○ B. A butcher might have had a pig-shaped weather vane.

○ C. Long ago, it was much windier than it is now.

Bags on a Belt

The Hongs followed the signs. Soon they found the baggage section. After a short wait, the large belt began to move. The Hongs watched as different bags went by. Other passengers grabbed their bags and left. At last, Maggie saw her family's luggage. She helped her parents take their bags off the belt. Then they all headed for the exit.

2. Which sentence is most likely true?

○ A. The Hongs lost their luggage.

○ B. The Hongs are starting a trip.

○ C. The Hongs are at an airport.

Name_____   Date_____

Read each paragraph. Then fill in the bubble
that best answers each question.

Samplers of the Past

About 300 years ago sewing was a school subject for girls. In those days, women and girls sewed all their own clothes. So girls learned to make different kinds of stitches. They tried out their stitches on a piece of cloth called a sampler. As the girls learned a stitch, they used it in a design. Some samplers had flowers or animals. Others showed scenes from daily life. Still others had verses from the Bible.

1. Which sentence is most likely true?

  ○ A. Long-ago samplers were made for fun.

  ○ B. Long-ago samplers were made for practice.

  ○ C. Long-ago samplers were made to wear.

Happy Birthday

It was Norm's birthday. He sat at the table, surrounded by his family. In front of him was a pile of gifts. Eagerly, he reached for the first package. It was a shirt from his aunt. Norm admired the gift and thanked her. Then he opened the other gifts. Each time, he smiled and said "thank you." The last box was a computer game. Norm yelled in delight, got up, and gave his grandmother a big hug.

2. Which sentence is most likely true?

  ○ A. Norm liked the shirt from his aunt best of all.

  ○ B. Norm really wanted the computer game.

  ○ C. Norm's family was not very generous.

Practice Page 22

Name_____ Date_____

Read each paragraph. Then fill in the bubble
that best answers each question.

A Book Story

Thomas Rockwell wrote a book called *How to Eat Fried Worms*. Did he ever eat a worm? Rockwell thought he probably should. He decided that if the book got published, he would eat a worm. Somehow he never found the time. Rockwell did talk to a doctor about worms though. Are they safe to eat? The doctor said worms are good for people.

1. **Which sentence is most likely true?**

   ○ A. Rockwell probably didn't want to eat a worm.

   ○ B. Rockwell hoped the doctor would buy his book.

   ○ C. Rockwell was sure that readers wouldn't eat worms.

What's the Time?

A faint light came from the East. Slowly, it spread over the town. One by one, the street lamps went out. Traffic noises began to pick up. Runners made their way along paths by the river. The first workers hurried to cars and trains. Students appeared to climb onto waiting buses. People put on glasses to protect their eyes from the rising sun.

2. **Which sentence is most likely true?**

   ○ A. It is early morning.

   ○ B. It is early evening.

   ○ C. It is late morning.

Name_____ Date_____

Read each paragraph. Then fill in the bubble
that best answers each question.

Looking at Laws

Governments make laws when a community
needs them. Sometimes laws made in the
past seem silly today. For
example, it is not lawful to
tickle a girl in Norton,
Virginia. If you go to Maine,
be sure to tie your
shoelaces. It is against the
law to have them undone.
And don't sneeze on trains
in West Virginia. You will be breaking the law.

1. Which sentence is most likely true?

○ A. All communities have the same laws.

○ B. Silly laws help people behave well.

○ C. The reasons for laws change over time.

☆ ☆ ☆

A Question for José

José gazed out the window. He could
hear the second graders on the
playground. It sounded like they were having
fun. José wished he could be with them. But
someone was saying his name. Quickly, José
looked at the front of the room. His face got
red, and he shook his head. No, he hadn't
heard the question.

**2. Which sentence is
most likely true?**

○ A. José is on the
playground.

○ B. José is studying
at home.

○ C. José is in a
classroom.

Practice Page 24

Name_____ Date_____

Read each paragraph. Then fill in the bubble
that best answers each question.

Frog Features

Did you know that frogs can fly? In
Asia some frogs have webbed feet
that act like parachutes. South
America has poison frogs. One of these
can kill 20,000 mice! Frogs in Europe
have lived to be almost 40 years old.
Frogs in Africa can be as big as
footballs. And in North America some
frogs freeze during the winter. They
thaw out again in the spring!

1. **Which sentence is most
   likely true?**
   ○ A. Frogs are alike no
       matter where they live.

   ○ B. Frogs can be found on
       many continents.

   ○ C. Frogs can fly from
       continent to continent.

Ali's List

Ali made a list of the things he
needed. He started with his water
bottle. Then he added gloves. Next came
shorts, shoes, and a helmet. "Don't forget
your fanny pack," said his sister. So Ali
wrote that on the list. He also added lunch.
His mother had promised to make him a
sandwich for the trip.

2. **Which sentence is
   most likely true?**
   ○ A. Ali is going to a
       football game.

   ○ B. Ali is going on a
       hiking trip.

   ○ C. Ali is going on a
       biking trip.

Name_____ Date_____

Read each paragraph. Then fill in the bubble
that best answers each question.

Long Ago News

Long ago there was no TV. No one had a radio. There were no computers. And there were very few newspapers. How did people get news? One way was from a town crier. This person walked through the streets and called out the news. If something special happened, the town crier beat a drum or rang a bell. People would run to hear the news.

1. **Which sentence is most likely true?**

   ○ A. There were few ways to get news long ago.

   ○ B. Most news in the past appeared in print.

   ○ C. In the past, people weren't interested in news.

Helping Lena

Lena woke up from a long nap. She tried to sit up, but it was too much trouble. Her mother came into the room. She had a tray with some juice on it. She patted the pillows and smoothed the sheets. Then she helped Lena sit up. "Try to drink this," said Lena's mom. "It's good for you."

2. **Which sentence is most likely true?**

   ○ A. Lena is a patient in a hospital.

   ○ B. Lena is sick in bed at home.

   ○ C. Lena had a bad nightmare.

Practice Page **26**

Name_____ Date_____

Read each paragraph. Then fill in the bubble
that best answers each question.

The First Sailors

The first sailors were amazed at some of the creatures they saw. They didn't know what these strange animals were. They thought that whales were monsters. They thought that lizards were dragons. As a result, mapmakers began to put monsters and dragons on the edges of maps. They believed that these fearful creatures came from places no one had yet explored.

1. **Which sentence is most likely true?**

   ○ A. The first sailors had seen whales and lizards in books.

   ○ B. People were afraid of things they didn't know about.

   ○ C. Early mapmakers could identify all places on the globe.

John Decides

John turned the pages slowly. He looked at all the pictures. Sometimes he read the text below them. John noted the prices of things too. Finally, he made up his mind. He went to the phone and dialed. Then John explained what he wanted.

2. **Which sentence is most likely true?**

   ○ A. John is reading a library book.

   ○ B. John is looking at a photo album.

   ○ C. John is ordering from a catalog.

Practice Page 27 Name_____ Date_____

Read each paragraph. Then fill in the bubble
that best answers each question.

Meet Princess

Princess sat in the sun. Lazily,
she licked her beautiful striped
fur. Then she rose and padded over to
her scratching post. It was the trunk
of a big tree. After sharpening her
claws, Princess played with her ball.
It was the size of a pumpkin. Then
Princess batted at her favorite toy. It
was an old tire hanging from the
tree. When she was thirsty, Princess
drank from her pool.

1. Which sentence is most likely true?

○ A. Princess is a household cat.

○ B. Princess is a zoo tiger.

○ C. Princess lives in the wild.

Mmmm . . .

Mrs. Plum took a small bag from the
cupboard. She placed it in the
microwave oven. While the oven was on,
Mrs. Plum got a bowl. A few minutes later,
Mrs. Plum opened the oven and took out the
bag. It was much bigger now. Mrs. Plum
emptied the contents of the bag into the
bowl. Then she added some salt. Mmmm. It
smelled good!

2. Which sentence is most likely true?

○ A. Mrs. Plum is baking cookies.

○ B. Mrs. Plum is making popcorn.

○ C. Mrs. Plum is heating leftovers.

Name_____ **Date**_____

Read each paragraph. Then fill in the bubble
that best answers each question.

In Minnesota

Minnesota is in the northern part of the U.S. This state has more than 10,000 lakes. Most of them freeze by December. People sometimes drive on the lakes then. During the winter the city of St. Paul has a big carnival. One event is an ice-carving contest. In Minneapolis, people use skywalks to go from building to building. That way they don't have to go outside in winter.

1. Which sentence is most likely true?

○ A. Minnesota has very cold winters.

○ B. Minnesota has no sidewalks or roads.

○ C. People carve ice in Minnesota's lakes.

☆ — ☆ — ☆

Ziggy and Dad

As they entered the park, Ziggy could see the horses. She asked her dad to hurry. She wanted to ride on her favorite horse. After her dad bought tickets, Ziggy ran to her horse and took the reins. Her dad helped her up. Then he climbed on the horse next to Ziggy. Soon the music began. Ziggy smiled and enjoyed her ride.

2. Which sentence is most likely true?

○ A. Ziggy is visiting a horse farm.

○ B. Ziggy is on a merry-go-round.

○ C. Ziggy is taking riding lessons.

Name_____ Date_____

Read each paragraph. Then fill in the bubble
that best answers each question.

Your Hair

A haircut doesn't hurt. But if someone pulls your hair, then you feel pain. That's because your hair is being pulled from its roots. The roots are the only parts of your hair that are alive and growing. The roots of your hair are under your skin. The roots are surrounded by nerves. Nerves sense pain.

1. Which sentence is most likely true?

○ A. The strands of your hair have no nerves.

○ B. Pain makes your hair grow quickly.

○ C. Getting a haircut is bad for the roots.

About Anna

A nna took off her shoes. She stood straight with her back against the wall. Anna's mother put the ruler on Anna's head and made a little mark on the wall. It was two inches above another mark. Next to the new mark, Anna's mother wrote the date. "Wow!" she said. "No wonder your jeans are too short."

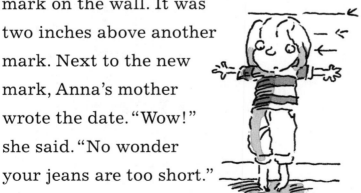

2. Which sentence is most likely true?

○ A. Anna's mother is measuring Anna's head.

○ B. Anna's mother is mad at Anna.

○ C. Anna has grown two inches taller.

Practice Page 30 Name_____ Date_____

Read each paragraph. Then fill in the bubble
that best answers each question.

What Tears Do

Sometimes tears are a sign of sadness. But tears have other jobs as well. Tears come from glands at the upper, outer part of the eye. Tears collect dust and germs that get into eyes. Tears then move through tiny tubes called ducts. They take the dust and germs with them. Sometimes tears may drip down your cheeks even if you're not crying.

1. **Which sentence is most likely true?**

   ○ A. Tears make your eyes dirty.

   ○ B. Dust and germs make you sad.

   ○ C. Tears keep your eyes clean.

Dave in School

Dave listened as his classmates answered the questions. He couldn't follow what they were saying. It was hard because he hadn't done the homework. Then the teacher asked another question. No one raised a hand. Dave slid down in his seat. He stared hard at his book. He covered part of his face with his hands.

2. **Which sentence is most likely true?**

   ○ A. Dave is a good student.

   ○ B. Dave doesn't know the answer.

   ○ C. Dave wants to be called on.

Practice Page 31

Name_____ Date_____

Read each paragraph. Then fill in the bubble
that best answers each question.

Home in a Castle

Long ago, most kings lived in castles. Castles were often built on steep hills. Their walls were high and very thick. Some castles had secret tunnels. People used the tunnels to escape if enemies came. Many castles also had moats around them. These were ditches filled with water. To enter a castle, visitors had to go over a bridge that was let down on chains. They then went through an entrance with a spiked gate.

1. **Which sentence is most likely true?**

   ○ A. It was easy to get inside a castle.

   ○ B. Castles were built for protection.

   ○ C. Everyone was welcome at a castle.

You've Got Mail!

Suki got an e-mail from her friend. The message made Suki happy. She went to talk to her mother. Then she checked the calendar. When she finished her homework, Suki wrote back to her friend. The answer was "Yes!"

2. **Which sentence is most likely true?**

   ○ A. The friend sent greetings to Suki's mother.

   ○ B. The friend asked about some homework.

   ○ C. Suki made a date to see her friend.

Practice Page 32   Name_____   Date_____

Read each paragraph. Then fill in the bubble
that best answers each question.

The Giant Cactus

A giant cactus grows in the desert. By the time the cactus is 150 years old, it is full of holes. In one hole lives a bat. Another hole is home to some insects. Birds lay eggs and raise families in the cactus, too. Even some pack rats find a place to live in the cactus. When one animal leaves the cactus, other ones move in.

1. **Which sentence is most likely true?**

   ○ A. The animals are harmful to the cactus.

   ○ B. The cactus provides a safe home for animals.

   ○ C. Only flying animals live in the cactus.

The Drink Machine

It was hot, and Mr. Santos was thirsty. He went down to the basement of the building. He found the drink machine. But Mr. Santos didn't have the right change. He went upstairs and got it. Then he went back to the machine. In went his quarters. Nothing happened. Mr. Santos pressed the coin return. Nothing. He banged on the machine. Nothing. He even kicked the machine. Still nothing.

2. **Which sentence is most likely true?**

   ○ A. Mr. Santos is losing his temper.

   ○ B. Mr. Santos is no longer thirsty.

   ○ C. Mr. Santos will fix the machine.

Practice Page **33**

Name_____ Date_____

Read each paragraph. Then fill in the bubble
that best answers each question.

New Cars

I t was the year 1903. Cars were still a pretty new product. They didn't look the way they do today. For example, when it rained, drivers couldn't see through the windshield. Instead, they had to lean their heads out the window. That gave Mary Anderson an idea. Her invention solved the problem and kept drivers dry.

1. Which sentence is most likely true?

○ A. Mary Anderson invented special car umbrellas.

○ B. Mary Anderson invented convertible cars.

○ C. Mary Anderson invented windshield wipers.

Kate's Meal

K ate was having dinner in a restaurant. She decided to order something different. When her meal came, Kate took a big bite. It was good. But then Kate's eyes opened wide. She began to cough. Her face turned red. Tears rolled down her cheeks. Quickly, Kate grabbed a glass of water and drank it down. She asked for another.

2. Which sentence is most likely true?

○ A. Kate ate something hot and spicy.

○ B. Kate is suddenly very sad.

○ C. Kate ordered a very sweet dessert.

Practice Page 34

Name_____ Date_____

Read each paragraph. Then fill in the bubble
that best answers each question.

State Nicknames

Each state has a nickname. These names reflect something special about the state. For example, New Hampshire is called the Granite State. That's because granite, a kind of rock, comes from New Hampshire. The nickname for Washington is the Evergreen State. Washington has lots of evergreen trees. Florida is often called the Sunshine State.

1. **Which sentence is most likely true?**
   - ○ A. Most days in Florida are very cloudy.
   - ○ B. Florida is known for its good weather.
   - ○ C. Florida has no special trees or rocks.

Papers From Mrs. Pence

Mrs. Pence stood at the front of the room. Everyone watched her. Then she began to call out names. One by one, the students stepped forward and got a paper. Some students smiled in relief. Others looked upset. Tina waited. When her name was called, she held her breath. Then she looked at her paper. Thank goodness she had studied!

2. **Which sentence is most likely true?**
   - ○ A. Tina will have to come in after school.
   - ○ B. Mrs. Pence is assigning homework.
   - ○ C. Tina did well on the recent test.

Name_____ Date_____

Read each paragraph. Then fill in the bubble
that best answers each question.

Pets and Presidents

Many U.S. presidents have had pets. Thomas Jefferson had a mockingbird. Zachary Taylor had a horse. Calvin Coolidge had a dog and a cat. Gerald Ford had a dog named Liberty. Franklin D. Roosevelt's dog was Fala. William Howard Taft had a cow that lived in the garage!

1. **Which sentence is most likely true?**

   ○ A. U.S. presidents like animals better than people.

   ○ B. The White House is no place for animals.

   ○ C. Pets are welcome at the White House.

Cookies in the Kitchen

When Mai and Tad came home, they smelled something delicious. Sure enough, there was a plate of homemade cookies on the kitchen table. Mai helped herself to a cookie. Then she took another. Tad had some too. The two of them sat in the kitchen talking. The smell of cookies brought Dad into the kitchen. He looked very disappointed when he saw the empty plate.

2. **Which sentence is most likely true?**

   ○ A. Dad didn't like the cookies.

   ○ B. Mai and Tad ate all the cookies.

   ○ C. Dad made the cookies for the kids.

Assessment 1   Name_____   Date_____

Read each paragraph. Then fill in the bubble
that best answers each question.

Flowing Rivers

Have you ever noticed that a ball always rolls downhill? So does water. That is because of gravity. So rivers can flow north or south. They can flow east or west. But they always flow from high places to lower places. The map shows the Nile River in Egypt. This river flows north. It goes into the Mediterranean Sea.

1. In what part of Egypt is the land the highest?

    _____

2. Why does the Nile River flow north?

    _____

    _____

A Rope Pull

The teams got in place. Then the coach gave the signal. The students began to pull on the rope. First one team tugged harder. Then the other team did. Suddenly, everyone was on the ground.

3. Why did the students fall down?

    _____

    _____

4. Why might the students be all dirty?

    _____

    _____

    _____

Assessment 2

Name_____ Date_____

Read each paragraph. Then fill in the bubble
that best answers each question.

How Clothes Help

How do clothes keep you warm?
Clothes keep you from losing
body heat. That's because clothes
trap air. The heat from your body
cannot get through the air. Snow
works in the same way. It traps lots
of air. People lost in winter storms
sometimes dig holes in the snow.
This helps them keep warm.

1. Why do people wear layers of
   clothes in the winter?

   _____

2. Why do people wear less clothing
   in warm temperatures?

   _____

   _____

The Shopping List

Ms. Burrows was going to
the supermarket. After she
got in the car, she remembered her
list. It was in the kitchen. She went
back into the house to get the list.
When she returned, her dog
Brownie was in the back seat.

3. How did Brownie get into the car?

   _____

   _____

4. Why did Brownie get in?

   _____

   _____

Assessment 3

Name_____ Date_____

Read each paragraph. Then fill in the bubble
that best answers each question.

Shark Teeth

Sharks are the hunters of
the ocean. But sharks are
always losing their teeth. Their
teeth do not have strong roots.
So the teeth break and fall out
easily. Sharks can lose thousands
of teeth in a lifetime. Luckily,
sharks have as many as 20 rows of
teeth. When one falls out, another
moves up from the row behind.

1. Why do sharks need teeth?

_____

2. Where might divers find lots of
shark teeth?

_____

On the Rail Trail

Doug and Anna met on the rail
trail. Anna began to brag about
her new skateboard. Doug got annoyed.
"A bike is better than a skateboard," he
said. Anna put her hands on her hips.
"Let's have a race," she said. "We'll see
which one is better."

1. Why does Anna suggest a race?

_____

2. Who will win the race? Why?

_____

_____

_____

Student Record Sheet

Name_____ Date _____

Date	Practice Page # _____	Number Correct	Comments

Answers

Page 8:
1. The movie was scary (or sad). He did not want to be alone because he was afraid (or felt upset).

2. He is reading the sports section. He might have cheered at the score because his team had won.

3. The men are firefighters. A firehouse has a pole that firefighters slide down and they hurry to their trucks to fight fires.

4. She broke her leg. When you break a bone, you have a cast and use crutches.

Page 9:
1. C
2. B

Page 10:
1. A
2. B

Page 11:
1. A
2. C

Page 12:
1. B
2. B

Page 13:
1. C
2. B

Page 14:
1. A
2. B

Page 15:
1. C
2. B

Page 16:
1. B
2. C

Page 17:
1. A
2. C

Page 18:
1. B
2. A

Page 19:
1. A
2. B

Page 20:
1. C
2. B

Page 21:
1. C
2. B

Page 22:
1. C
2. C

Page 23:
1. B
2. B

Page 24:
1. B
2. A

Page 25:
1. A
2. A

Page 26:
1. B
2. C

Page 27:
1. B
2. A

Page 28:
1. B
2. C

Page 29:
1. B
2. B

Page 30:
1. A
2. A

Page 31:
1. C
2. C

Page 32:
1. B
2. C

Page 33:
1. A
2. B

Page 34:
1. B
2. C

Page 35:
1. B
2. B

Page 36:
1. A
2. B

Page 37:
1. A
2. C

Page 38:
1. C
2. B

Page 39:
1. B
2. C

Page 40:
1. B
2. A

Page 41:
1. C
2. A

Page 42:
1. B
2. C

Page 43:
1. C
2. B

Page 44:
Possible answers:
1. The land is highest in the southern part of Egypt.

2. The Nile flows north because it flows from higher land to lower land.

3. One team pulled back hard enough to bring the other team forward and they all fell down.

4. They fell onto the ground and got soil on them.

Page 45:
Possible answers:
1. They wear layers of clothes to trap layers of air.

2. In warm weather you want to get rid of some body heat so you don't want to trap air.

3. Ms. Burrows left the car door open.

4. The dog wanted to go along.

Page 46:
Possible answers:
1. They need them for the food they hunt.

2. There are most likely lots of shark teeth on the ocean floor.

3. She has been challenged by Doug.

4. Doug will most likely win the race. A bike has larger wheels and is faster than a skateboard.